Marcel Duchamp and François Villon

Readymades Read and Made Part 3

Lyn Merrington

ARE PRESS

ISBN: 978-0-6487276-4-4

DEDICATION

Cameron and Isabelle.

Contents

Acknowledgements

I would like to thank the University of Western Australia for its support and thank the University of Lille 3 for giving me exposure to living French language from 2003 to 2009.

I'd also like to thank all my French Friends, you know who you are, including the *petites grenouilles*, who have brought the language to life, with expressions that are not in dictionaries.

I'd like to thank my family for putting up with my seemingly permanent piles of books, and with my persistently imposing my French folly on them.

Thanks again to Professor Ian McLean.

Marcel Duchamp and François Villon

1

Marcel Duchamp and François Villon:

The family connection

The importance of the familial relationship between Marcel Duchamp and his older brothers was significant. Marcel (July 28, 1887-October 1 1968), was born Henri Robert Marcel. His older brothers, Jacques Villon (July 31, 1875 – June 9, 1963) and Raymond Duchamp Villon, (5 November 1876 - 9 October 1918), were born Gaston Emile Duchamp and Pierre-Maurice-Raymond Duchamp respectively. The influence of his brothers was key, both in terms of Marcel's psychological and artistic development. The 12 and 11 years that separated Marcel from them meant that they were important role models, but also that they were separated by generational change. His relationship with them was not only paramount for his early development, but was seminal in the chain of events which led to the formation of his subsequent radical attitudes to art and the artworld. Given these simple facts, it would seem and examination of the figure whom Marcel's brothers renamed themselves after, François Villon, would be long overdue.

Pierre Cabanne, in his comprehensive study *Les Frères Duchamp*, indicates the brothers' shared attitude to art, despite their radically different approaches. Jacques Villon said "Art is the expression of some basic truth, not a romantic outpouring". Cabanne says all the brothers shared this opinion.[1] Marcel Duchamp is well known for his many statements emphasising the intellectual content of art in preference to what he called the retinal in art, which he saw as at its zenith in impressionism. In a 1964 interview with Calvin Tomkins when speaking of the contemporary ideas of art, and collectors Duchamp says disparagingly 'there's a great deal of traditionalism in collectors. They are not generally intelligent enough. They are feelers, not intellectuals.'[2] This statement is indicative of Duchamp's conception of the intellectual and emotional. He sees them as opposed, not as complementary, and much prefers

[1] Pierre Cabanne, *The Brothers Duchamp*, (Boston, New York Graphic society, 1976), 24

[2] Marcel Duchamp, "The Afternoon Interviews New York, 1964", Calvin Tomkins, *Marcel Duchamp, The Afternoon Interviews*, (New York: Badlands Unlimited, 2013), 27.

an intellectual approach to an emotional one.

“I like the word think” He told JJ Sweeney in 1955, “Generally, when people say I know they don’t, they think. I think that art is the only form of activity in which man can show himself as a real individual. By that alone he can transcend the animal stage because art is an opening into regions dominated neither by time nor space.’[3]

Duchamp’s opposition to the emotional extended also to other realms including music.

“I’m not anti-music. But I don’t get on with’ the ‘catgut’ side of it. You see, music is gut against gut: the intestines respond to the catgut of the violin. There’s a sort of intense sensory lament, of

[3] *Cabanne*, 1976, 91, from Interview by James Johnson Sweeney at Philadelphia Museum for film produced by National Broadcasting co. in 1955

sadness and joy, which corresponds to retinal painting, which I can't stand. For me music isn't a superior expression of the individual. I prefer poetry. And even painting, although that's not very interesting either.[4]

Marcel spent a lot of time with his brothers, as would be expected, both at home and then later when he followed them to Paris to pursue an artistic career as they were doing. Jacques Villon and Raymond Duchamp Villon moved to the Montmartre area of Paris in 1894, firstly for Jacques to study law, and Raymond to study medicine. Both, however, later dropped these studies for art. In 1906 they moved to the quieter,

---

[4] Duchamp, in Jennifer Gough Cooper, Jacques Caumont, *Marcel Duchamp Work and Life*, (Cambridge, Massachusetts, MIT Press, 1993), (Ephemerides), unpaginated, but organised by date only 1966, 1st July, London.

more isolated village of Puteaux on the outskirts of Paris. Cabanne describes Marcel as not liking being left at home in Normandy, in a feminine household, after his brothers left for Paris[5]. He followed his brothers to Paris in 1904 and enrolled in the Academie Julien, then dominated by the much respected and widely collected academic painter of sentimental works, Alphonse Bougereau. Marcel however preferred to play billiards in the local cafe than attend classes. In the spring of 1905, at the age of 17, he failed the entrance exam to the Ecole de Beaux arts, then the gateway to a career in art, a humiliation which may go some way to explaining his later skeptical attitude towards academic art and approval[6].

---

[5] Cabanne, 1976, 91.
[6] Calvin Tomkins, *Duchamp, a Biography*, (New York, Henry

Later, in May 1905, Duchamp cancelled his paid-up classes at the Academie Julien and enrolled as an art worker in the *Imprimerie de la Vicomte*, in Rouen, where his retired parents were living, as a loophole allowed artworkers to serve only one year instead of two of the military service that was compulsory for all Frenchmen. Five months later he took the exam for an *ouvrier d'art*, an artworker, and answered questions about Leonardo. For the practical component of the exam, "you had to show what you could do by way of printed engravings."[7] In what was perhaps his first 'readymade' Marcel had procured one of his maternal grandfather Emile Nicolle's copper plates of series *The Hundred Towers of Rouen*, and he

Holt and Company, 1996),32-33.

[7] Tomkins, 1996, 33

presented every member of the jury with prints he had pulled from this plate. He passed the exam with 49 out of 50 and then presented for military service on 3 October. He served in the town of Eu, not far from Rouen, was promoted to corporal in April and was discharged in October 1906.

He went straight back to Paris and rented an apartment at 65 Rue Caulaincourt, not far from his brothers' former flat in Montmartre. Downstairs, in his building, in the café-brasserie Manière, the circle of artist humorists met regularly. Humorists such as Adolphe Willette, Lucien Metivet, Théophile- Alexandre Steinlen, and Jean Louis Forain, were much admired minor celebrities, and could make good money. Duchamp often played billiards with the young Spaniard Juan Gris, already a friend of Picasso's, but he avoided Picasso himself. Both Gris and Duchamp took drawings to the offices of *Le Courrier Français The French mail*, and *Le Rire*, *Laughter*, but it was two years before either of them sold one drawing.

Marcel was on his own for the first time, as his brothers had recently moved to Puteaux. He visited them almost every Sunday where they played games such as *spiroballe* (a game with a ball on a string attached to a post) and enjoyed long lunches.[8]

Duchamp describes the atmosphere in his brother, Jacques Villon's house during this time:

« Oh! it was very simple, very familial firstly, but also mixed with the other cubists who came, at that time to Puteaux, where my brother [Jacques]

---

[8] Tomkins, 1996, 35.

has lived since 1905, I think. There were these kind of "Sundays at Puteaux" where everyone came; cubists of that period, La Fresnaye, Gleizes, Metzinger, Leger, amusing Sunday afternoons when we did archery, there was a garden, so it was nice, in summer especially. There were discussions, naturally, that were completely theoretical. It was a sort of agora. Those kinds of things are very edifying for young people. I was young, I was about twenty-four. It's really a very salutary source of inspiration, for a young man in any case. »[9]

---

[9] *Etant Donné, no. 6 Marcel Duchamp et John Cage*, Paris, 2005, 5 This text accompanies a photo of Marcel being hosed down, or *arrosé* in the garden at Jacques Villon's house in Puteaux. My translation.*"Oh ! C'était très simple très familial d'abord, mais aussi mélangé avec les autres cubistes qui venaient, à ce moment-là à Puteaux, ou mon frère habite depuis 1905, je crois. Il avait fait des sortes de « dimanches à Puteaux, » où tout le monde venait : des cubistes de cette époque, La Fresnaye, Gleizes, Metzinger, Leger, des après-midis de dimanche amusants ou l'on tirait à l'arc, il y'avait un jardin, donc c'etait agréable, en été surtout. Il s'en suivait*

Although the relations between Marcel and his brothers have been explored, to my knowledge the influence on Marcel Duchamp's work of François Villon, the writer after whom Gaston/ Jacques, Marcel's oldest brother, and then Jean-Philippe / Raymond, chose to name themselves, has not been explored.

The pseudonym that Marcel's brother Gaston chose is not insignificant; born Gaston, he chose, around 1897 when his first cartoon was published in the humorous journal *le Rire,* (*Laughter*) to change his name, as he didn't want his own surname 'to be bandied about in rather controversial publications

---

des discussions, naturellement, complètement théorique. C'était une sorte d'agora. Ces choses-là sont très édifiantes pour des jeunes gens. J'étais jeune, j'avais vingt-quatre ans, à peu près. C'est vraiment une source d'inspiration très salutaire, pour un jeune homme en tout cas. » This citation is not footnoted in *Etant Donné*.

that often poked fun at morality, religion and the army.'[10] He chose to name himself Jacques Villon after the Mediaeval French poet Francois Villon. This was a strategic act, the reference to the well known Francois Villon, giving him a link to the larrikin and perhaps an air of disrespect. After this, Raymond, the second brother, also changed his name to Villon, but chose to also hyphenate the family name Duchamp, to Duchamp-Villon, as he wanted to distinguish himself from his older brother by signing Duchamp-Villon.

Given the name his brothers chose in preference to the family name, it seems probable that Marcel Duchamp was familiar with Francois Villon's life

---

[10]Cabanne, 1976, 10 Cabanne notes it was family tradition to change names as Duchamp's father had changed his name from Isidore Justin to Eugène.

story, and with at least some of his work. Villon's work, which is characterised as showing humour, parody and irreverence, is worth looking at, at least cursorily in the context of any study of Duchamp, as these are qualities which are evident, if not dominant, in Duchamp's oeuvre.

Francois Villon is recognised as one of the poets who brought the vernacular into his poetry. He has been called arguably the greatest poet of the poets of *argot*, slang[11] or *langue verte* (literally green language). This cannot be an insignificant element of the milieu in which Marcel Duchamp developed his language skills, his sense of humour, his taste, and his methodology, with his use of *langue verte* or slang.

---

[11] *Larousse Dictionnaire du Français argotique et populaire*, Francois Caradec, (Paris : Larousse, 2006), 268

Much of what we know of François Villon is from his own texts, as they are all based on his life and personal history.

2

Francois Villon's Life

It is now accepted that François Villon was born François de Montcorbier, in Paris, in 1431, but in the 1877 Edition of Villon's complete works, the biography available in 'Jacques Villon's' youth, Montcorbier was named as an associate of Villon, not Villon himself. By 1910 Villon's birth name was identified as Montcorbier or Des Loges[12]. We know from his own text that Villon had an illiterate

[12] Gaston Paris, *Les Grands Ecrivains Français, François Villon*, (Paris, Librairie Hachette, 1910), 15. Paris says Villon probably came from a Bourbonnais town that no longer exists.

mother,

Femme je suis povrette et ancienne, Ne riens ne sçay; oncques lettre ne leuz;

Woman I am poor and old, Know nothing, no letter having read.[13]

He was probably orphaned of his father who was possibly a tradesman, perhaps a *cordouennier* (a leatherworker)[14]. He was certainly from a poor family as is written in his Grand Testament, verse XXXV.

Pauvre je suys de ma jeunesse

Poor I am from my youth

---

[13] Le Monnoye Edition, « Grand Testament », *Oeuvres Complètes de François Villon*, (Paris, Marpon et Flammarion, 1881),55, mise à jour avec notes et glossaire par Pierre Jannet. This Edition is the principal reference for the online Gutenberg Project Edition of Villon's works, and was widely considered to be a reliable Edition *Ballade que Villon feit a la requeste de sa mere pour prier notre dame.*

[14] Pierre Jannet, in La Monnoye Edition, preface, vii.

De pauvre et de petite extrace.

Of poor and little extraction

Mon pere n'eut oncq grand richesse.

My father had no great riches

Ne son ayeul, nommé Erace.

Nor did his elder called Erace

Pauvreté tous nous suyt et trace.

Poverty follows and traces us.[15]

Villon still had some ill feeling towards his own relatives, as is indicated in his Grand Testament

Des miens le moindre, je di voir

Of my own the least, I say I've seen

[15] Project Gutenberg, and 1881 La Monnoye Edition, 31. My translation.

De me desavouver s'avance,

To disavow me in advance

Oubliant naturel devoir

Forgetting natural obligation

Par faute d'un peu de chevance.

For lack of a little wealth.[16]

As was common at the time for children who showed some aptitude, Villon was placed in the care of the church and lived under the care of maître Guillaume de Villon, an influential and important chaplain in the church of Saint Benoit le Bétourné, in Paris, whose name he took in 1456. Francois obtained a bachelor's degree, and then a

[16] Gaston Paris, 16, This citation is not footnoted, but is on 28 of the 1881 Le Monnoye Edition, and on 28 of the 1877 (Lacroix) Prompsault edition. Spelling in the last two editions is as follows *Mes miens le moindre, je dy voir/De me desadvouer s'avance, /Oubliant naturel devoir, / Par faulte d'ung peu de chevance.'*

Maitrise des Arts, in 1452 at age 21, which gave him the status of *clerc*[17]. *Clercs* did not receive remuneration and Francois was involved in many disputes. The chaplain's influence protected him, but on 5 June 1455 he killed a priest, ostensibly in self-defence, and he fled Paris in fear of justice.[18] Villon received his letters of remission 7 months later, in January 1456, due to Guillaume de Villon's influence, and the fact that the priest who had been killed pardoned him before his death. On reception of his letters of remission Villon returned to Saint Benoit in Paris[19].

In Christmas of the same year he and some

---

[17]Pierre Champion, Vol .1, 39,

[18] Champion, Vol. 2, 10-12. For detailed account of this incident.

[19] Champion, Vol 2, 15-16, Champion says it was very rare for a murder conviction to be pardoned and this was due to his previous good record.

acquaintances robbed the coffers of the College of Navarre, and Villon left Paris, well before the theft was discovered several months later, in March 1457. Before fleeing Paris, Villon wrote what is now known as *Le Petit Testament*, giving the reasons for his flight as a *chagrin d'amour*.

The 1877 Edition recounts in a footnote, the confession of one of Villon's companions who also said that Villon had left Paris to rob a monk who had 500 écus.[20] Gaston Paris' 1910 publication contains a detailed account of the robbery of the College de Navarre, including details of the confession of Guy Tabarie, one of Villon's associates.[21]

There is some discrepancy between accounts of

[20] 1877 Edition, fnote xx. recounts confession of Guy Tabarie.
[21] Gaston Paris, 55-57

what happened to Villon over the next few years. Some accounts say he wandered the country, others that he was in Paris.[22]

Several accounts say he was arrested for theft, in 1457, and he was condemned to death. However he appealed it, and unlike his companions, some of whom were hung, was pardoned on the birth of a Princess, Marie d'Orléans, in 1457, for whom he wrote some moving verse, winning the favour of her father, the poet Charles d'Orleans, in whose

[22] Pierre Jannet in the 1881 Edition (and Proj Gutenberg) says that in 1457 Villon was in the prisons of Chatelet, and le parlement, after having submitted the *question des eaux* (made to drink boiling water) and condemned to death. It says he was pardoned on the birth of Charles D'Orléans daughter in Dec 1457, due to Charles D'Orléans influence. The 1877 Edition says Villon was in prison in Paris several times and condemned for '*vol nocturne a main armée sur les grands chemins*', armed highway robbery at night, though this is not dated in this Edition xxiij. Wikipedia says Villon left Paris of his own accord near Xmas 1456 and wandered for several years. Gaston Paris 1910 edition, 57 speculates that Villon did not return to Paris for several years after his voyage to Angers.

court he spent some time and in whose books several of his ballades are contained, probably written in Villon's own hand.[23]

Villon was again condemned, for some crime, that he himself attributes, in his *Débat du coeur et du corps de Villon, Debate of the heart and body of Villon*, written in the prison of Meung-sur-Loire, to his *folle plaisance*, crazy pleasure- (perhaps slander or sacrilege). He was detained by the bishop of Orléans, and pardoned, as was customary, on the visit of the newly ordained King Louis XI to the town of Meung-sur-Loire, in 1461

[23] Pierre Champion paints a vivid picture of life on the road and robberies which were common at that time, He places the writing of the poem to Charles D'Orleans daughter on her entry to Orleans, 3 years after her birth, not in 1457. Gert Pinkernell, *Francocis Villon et Charles D'Orléans* Heidelberg press 1992, states that it was probably Villon himself who transcribed his poems into Charles D'Orléans *Recueill* of *Dits*. 12. he dates this at some time after 1450 when the *Recueil* was started.

where he had been incarcerated.[24] Gaston Paris' 1910 study of Villon's life and work attributes his incarcerations in Meung to a robbery for which he was arrested at Baccon[25].

Accounts of Villon's life after this vary. The 1877 edition says he was pardoned but his sentence was commuted to banishment and that he had to leave France, going to England for some time. The same Edition draws on Rabelais' writing which recounts him being welcomed in England by Edward IV, and also writing verse for parishioners in France. This edition says he lived until 1483.[26] The 1881 Edition

---

[24] Pierre Jannet, Preface, *Oeuvres completes de Francois Villon, Gutenberg Project*, x. Villon rails against Thibault d'Aussigny, Bishop of Orléans whom he says has judged him falsely. Villon did not complain about his first condemnation and whipping, so Jannet considers there is good reason for Villon to complain about this injustice.

[25] Gaston Paris, 1910, 8.

[26] Edition 1877, fnotes, xxiv, for banishment, xxxiv for Rableais recounting story of Etienne Tappecoue, and also for Villon

with preface by Jannet refers to Rabelais writings also and says Rabelais' account is not verifiable but possible[27]. Pierre Champion in *François Villon, Sa vie et son temps* shows that Rabelais' accounts are not possibly true, but that he knew Villon's writing well, citing it.[28]

---

playing the Passion '*en gestes et languaige poictevin.*'

[27] Pierre Jannet, notes et introduction *Les oeuvres complètes de François Villon,* Gutenberg project, 7 '*Enfin, Rabelais, livre IV, chapitre XIII, nous apprend que «maistre François Villon, sus ses vieux jours, se retira à*
Saint-Maixent en Poictou, sous la faveur d'un homme de bien, abbé dudit lieu. Là, pour donner passe-temps au peuple, entreprit faire jouer la Passion en gestes et langage poictevin [24]. » *Ce témoignage n'est pas irrécusable ; mais pourquoi ne pas l'accepter ? Après une vie aussi agitée, on aime à se représenter le pauvre poète enfin tranquille, à l'abri du besoin, s'occupant, pour son plaisir, de jeux dramatiques, auxquels il avait dû probablement, dans d'autres temps, demander son pain* [25].

[28] Pierre Champion, François *François Villon sa vie et son temps,* (Paris: Honore Chapion, 1913)248-52. Champion shows that the dates in which Rabelais places Villon in France are not possible as King Edward V was killed at 13 yrs of age, not living to a ripe old age as Rabelais says, and the doctor Linacre, whom Rabelais says served him did not serve him, Champion asks if Rabelais is teasing in putting in these dates which he

Gaston Paris' 1910 study recounts Villon's return to Paris before 1462 when he wrote his ballades in the jargon of the *coquillards*, who were wandering, but organised robbers, thus named as they wore *coquilles,* shells, on their hats to look like pilgrims. He says Villon was in prison in Chatelet early in November 1462, and was released, probably because of his Royal pardon of 1461, which should have pardoned him for all previous crimes. On interrogation he admitted the theft of the college of Navarre and agreed to pay back 120 écus to the church, over 3 years, showing he still had the support of people who were solvent. After his release he was in the company of some people who were in a dispute and was again arrested, and put to the *question des eaux*, the question of the

---

must have known were wrong.

waters, a torture method, as his previous protector, Robert D'Estouteville was no longer Prevot de Paris[29].

Villon was, in his opinion, given a *peine arbitraire* an arbitrary sentence, He says *on me jugea par tricherie*, he was judged by trickery [30]. He was condemned to be hung and strangled. Gaston Paris says it was at this point that Villon wrote the *Ballade des Pendus, The Ballad of the Hung*, expecting to be hung. In this he asked those who will see him and his companions hung not to mock them as was the custom in those days, and asks for divine forgiveness. He appealed to parliament and was pardoned on 5 January 1463; his condemnation

---

[29] Gaston Paris, 68-70

[30] Villon « Ballade de L'appel de Villon » Gutenberg project, and La Monnoye edition, 1881, 104.

being considered excessive. However, due to his previous bad behaviour he was condemned to banishment from Paris, though not from France. He wrote a joyful verse to the clerk of the court celebrating the success of his appeal. He also asked for 3 days to gather some money and say goodbye to his family. This he was apparently granted[31].

We lose track of Villon, from here on, and as we have seen there are various speculations on the date of Villon's death.

---

[31] Gaston Paris, 71-72, an account of this is also in Champion, *vol 2*, 243-245

3

Villon's work, its reception and Marcel

Francois Villon broke with the tradition of allegory and affectation which reigned supreme at the time and is considered to be the first realist poet, introducing personal subject matter instead of the general or edifying poetry that had gone before him. He understood the courtly forms of poetry but reversed the themes and values and celebrated the lowlifes destined for the gallows instead of praising high ideals. Indeed, Marcel's brother Gaston / Jacques' choice of Villon as a surname is described as having been 'in homage to the author of the *Ballade des pendus'*, the Ballad of the hung.[32]

Francois Villon did not enjoy literary success during his lifetime, as his work was not considered to be part of the solemn rhetorical literature of the time. He is not included in lists of eminent writers of the time.[33] His work was known orally and in the circles of *écoliers,* or university students, from which he came, and Marot later said that old people knew his work by heart. Hand-written copies of his work perhaps circulated as the printing process was not yet widespread[34]. His work

---

[32] Cabanne, 1976, 10.

[33] Gaston Paris, 170-171

[34] Gaston Paris, 163-164. Paris says we don't really know how works were known before the advent of printing in Paris though the early manuscript copies of some of his works are in *recueils composites*, composite collections, made for or by amateurs. He also says Villon could not have afforded to have copies of his works made for amateurs as was the custom for writers to do at that time. It is also highly unlikely that

was not published during his lifetime, the first dated edition being made in 1489.[35] However his deeds were part of legend, and were recounted, ostensibly by one of his acquaintances, in the *Repues Franches*. This text was described as 'a singular monument to his glory by one of his disciples, [which] makes known to us by which ingenious combinations and tricks he and his companions procured the means to lead a joyful life and obtain free meals. Their mischievousness was altogether within the morals of the time, and didn't exceed ...what we would willingly be tempted to call good tricks, but they were on a

---

amateurs of literature would have approved of him at that time.

[35] Prompsault identified a previous edition which was non-dated, but which was not in the Manuel de Librairie. *Oeuvres de François Villon* Préface par Paul Lacroix, Librairie des Bibliophiles, E Flammarion Successeur, 1877, viij,ix

slippery slope and justice didn't understand mockery.[36]

Villon was certainly widely and for a long time known as a trickster, his name having entered the language in several ways. "I say *villoneries* to express a trickster: we still use the name of this incorrigible deceitful person in saying he's a Villon, or he does nothing but villons."[37] In 1910 he was also known as a kind of archetype of the larrikin

---

[36] Jannet, 1881 Edition, Preface, viii *'singulier monument élevé a sa gloire par quelqu'un de ses disciples, nous font connaitre par quelles combinaisons ingénieuses lui et ses compagnons se procuraient les moyens de mener joyeuse vie. Leurs friponneries, étaient tout à fait dans les mœurs du temps, et ne dépassaient sans doute pas les proportions de ce qu'on serait volontiers tenté d'appeler des bons tours ; mais ils étaient sur une pente glissante, et la justice n'entendait pas raillerie.'*

[37] Colletet, « Preface », *Œuvres de François Villon*, Librairie de bibliophiles, Flammarion, Paris, 1877, xxxj. *'je dy villonneries pour exprimer un trompeur : on se sert encore du nom de ce fourbe fieffe, en disant « C'est un Villon » ou il ne fait que villonner »*

poor man, the expression '*pauvre comme Villon*' as poor as Villon, becoming a kind of proverb[38].

The first edition of Villon's work, in 1489, was a great success and it was reprinted more than 20 times until the next edition appeared in 1533. This was prepared by Clément Marot for François 1er, who was said to have appreciated Villon's work.[39] Villon went out of favour with the École de Ronsard et la Pleiade, but was admired by La Fontaine, Voltaire and many writers of the C17 and C18. He has come back into favour since with many interpretations having been made of his works and life[40].

---

[38] Gaston Paris, 171.

[39] Gaston Paris, 171

[40] Jannet, *Œuvres completes de Francois Villon*, Gutenberg project, 9 Jannet also cites M.A. de Montaiglon's analysis of Villon's works and importance.

François Villon's story of academic disapproval during his lifetime and then later success is echoed in Duchamp's career pathway. Duchamp's work is now well known for being rejected several times during his lifetime by the art establishment, (in 1912 by his brothers and the Cubists, and in 1917 by the committee of the Society of Independent Artists). However, he has since come back into favour among the cognoscenti of the art world, however not generally with the public at large. He was recently cited, in a 2004 survey of artists, curators and art dealers, as the most influential artist of the twentieth century and has become a reference point[41].

---

[41] Perlman, B. Bennard "Font of inspiration" *Art and Antiques*, Sept 2005, vol. 28 Issue 9, 70-73, A December 2004 survey of 500 British artists curators, critics and art dealers, named Duchamp's *Fountain* as the most influential work of modern

It may have been reassuring for Duchamp to have known the history of Villon's reception, and it may have influenced the development of his ideas about history and posterity. His well-known statements about the role of the onlooker or the spectator in the making of history echo the history of the reception of Villon's work, which became part of the 'history of French literature' due to its appeal to so many people, rather than academic approval at the time of his life.

Duchamp said "As far as art history is concerned we know that in spite of what the artist has said or did, something stayed on that was completely independent of what the artist desired; it was grabbed by society, which made it its own. The artist doesn't count" ..."The artist produces

---

art.

nothing until the onlooker has said "You have produced something marvellous" The onlooker has the last word"[42] "if there is no onlooker there is no art, is there? ... I give to the onlooker more importance than the artist'[43]

Duchamp was also very aware of the revisions of history that take place, as they did with Villon's work 'when a million people look at a painting they change it by looking alone...[s]ometimes it's an embellishment. With El Greco... it became a rebirth hundred years ago. He had been buried long ago, two or three centuries... but he will probably deteriorate again after two centuries of admiration.'[44] 'The same thing with my damn

---

[42] Duchamp in Tomkins, 2013, 30-31.
[43] Duchamp in Tomkins, 2013, 56.
[44] Duchamp in Tomkins, 2013, 60

Nude...from a scandalous painting it became a boring painting, by being looked at so much." Oh that's the Nude again." [laughs] It's detrimental to the poor thing.'[45]

At the time of the Duchamp's youth, research was being done into Villon's life story and new documents were being discovered[46]. Most significant of researchers of the time were M Longnon who discovered important documents, including those recounting the theft of the College de Navarre, and reconstituted Villon's life with a study published in 1892. Marcel Schwob's studies of Villon were also made available to several writers who published work on Villon.[47] Villon was in

---

[45] Duchamp in Tomkins, 2013, 61.

[46] Gaston Paris, 167.

[47] Gaston Paris, 168. Schwob made his notes available to Paris, and they were available to Pierre Champion for his study

fashion, and had been admired by many writers including Banville, Baudelaire and Verlaine, and English writers, including Swinburne. The English poet and painter Dante Gabriel Rossetti was central to the creation of the Villon society[48]. In 1878 the poet John Payne translated all of his works into English.

As we have seen, even if we cannot be sure of exactly which details of Villon's life and work the Duchamps were familiar, François Villon was certainly well known, and known to have been a larrikin, a thief and a killer by 1912, the year in which Marcel and his brothers significant dispute took place. It is, in my opinion, extremely unlikely

---

Francois Villon sa vie et son temps.
[48] Gaston Paris, 185.

that the Duchamp / Villons were unaware of contemporary research into François Villon's work.

It was Villon's namesake, Marcel's brother, Jacques Villon who announced the cubists' disapproval of his work, *Nude descending a staircase #2*, to him.

> "Gleizes... found the painting offensive and asked Jacques Villon and Raymond Duchamp-Villon to persuade their brother to withdraw it. They were upset: they put on black clothes and a funereal manner and went to see Duchamp, who complied with a smile, much to his visitors' relief, and left only a companion drawing to *Nude* at the Salon.[49]

[49] Pierre Cabanne, 1976, 68.

One can imagine Marcel seeing the irony and almost feel his derision when faced with this rejection of his work for being non-conformist, or offensive, as it was made by his brothers, Gaston / Jacques Villon and Raymond Duchamp Villon. They had chosen to name themselves after a radical nonconformist, Francois Villon, who clearly used vulgar language and portrayed subjects that would have been considered by many to be offensive in his time, and even to some of Duchamp's contemporaries.

Indeed, the depth of Marcel's disgust at this one event was to carry him for many years, 'to leave him with a feeling of rejection and bitterness that lingered for a long time' and direct the course of his career.[50] Of this event he said 'I didn't discuss it

[50] Calvin Tomkins, 2013, 8,9

with anyone, but it was really a turn in my life. I saw that I would never be very much interested in groups after that. I felt it was too much of a schooling.... to say you must do this and you must do that, very much of an academy attitude.'[51] This event made him 'very much a loner and someone who refused to participate in things other artists were doing and... reinforced his need for complete independence'[52]. However, the repercussions of this event have been explored elsewhere so we shall return to our examination of Francois Villon's work in relation to Duchamp.

---

[51] Duchamp, Tomkins, 2013, 71

[52] Calvin Tomkins,2013, 9.

4

The Everyday and The Vulgar

In looking at Francois Villon's oeuvre we see the subject matter, his own life, which at the time would not have been considered a worthy subject for art, and his methods are precursors to those of Duchamp. Villon does not limit himself to high minded or approved subjects but chooses his subjects from everyday life, just as Duchamp later chose to take his 'readymade' objects from everyday life and nominate them art.

One only has to cite a critique of François Villon's method of rhyming to see the breadth of his language. He has no compunction about using formal or elevated language in the same work as vulgar language. He even makes use of rhymes which juxtapose elevated language and elements with extremely vulgar language in a levelling that is almost a parody. Indeed, his rhyming technique has thrown into light his particular accent as it highlights his Parisian accent which makes these rhymes work, when other accents would not necessarily rhyme.

'If he makes *fuste* [a light and rapid type of boat] rhyme with *fusse*, [first person, imperfect subjunctive of the verb *être* to be], *prophètes* [prophets] with *fesses* [arse] it is again a question of

Parisian pronunciation'[53]. The use of the subjunctive in modern French is a marker of education and good language use. Villon often uses the subjunctive in his work, as would be required for good grammar, even though he usually speaks of the events of his life, rather than approved poetic subjects such as love and virtues, and peppers his verse with vulgar language. The effect of this is to highlight his irony and render his text comic.

Villon not only mixes different levels of language he also uses, in this particular instance, references to classical Greek culture in comparison to his own life. The first rhyme of *fuste* with *fusse* is in verse XVIII

[53] Gutenberg Project 13 M. A. de Montaiglon. '*S'il fait rimer fuste avec fusse, prophètes avec fesses [35], c'est encore une affaire de prononciation*', 1881 Edition remarques Philologiques, xxiv.

of the Grand testament where Villon complains that his life has been such because of his poverty.

Pourquoy larron me faiz nommer?
Why do you call me a scoundrel?
Pour ce qu'on me voit escumer
Because one sees me prowl about [54]
En une petite fuste ?
In a light boat
Se comme toy me peusse armer,
If like you I could arm myself
Comme toy empreur je fusse
As you are emperor I would be[55]

Villon uses the informal form of you, *toy, (*in modern French *toi)* when 'speaking' to the emperor, which one imagines would have been a too familiar form of address, showing a lack of respect.

The next verse contains his excuse for his behaviour

---

[54] *Dictionnaire de l'ancien français,* (Paris : Larousse, 1969) 1250 *escume- écume, mousse*, 1160,
[55] Kinnell, 37

Et sçaches qu'en grand pauvreté
And know that in great poverty
...
Ne gist pas trop grand loyaulté
There lies no great loyalty.

He sees his actions as the result of the fact that he was not saved from great poverty by a generous patron, as Diomedes was by Alexander[56]. He suggests that if he had been saved in such a way he may have behaved more valiantly.

The second example of Villon's rhymes cited above to illustrate his accent – rhyming *prophètes* (prophets) with *fesses* (arses) speaks in a down to

[56] Villon Grand Testament, XVIII rd verse of 8 lines, 1877 Edition, 27 the reference to Diomedes is in verse XX "*Ta fortune je mueray/ De mauvaise en bonne ! Luy dit. / SI fist-il. Onc puis ne mesdit / a personne, mais fut vray homme.* » Your fortune I'll change / from bad to good! He said/ so he did. Then never did misdeeds to anyone."

earth manner, using an idiomatic expression which foreshadows Duchamp's later use of such an expression. When speaking of the dead and entry to heaven, Villon makes reference to the exception made for patriarchs and prophets:

Toutesfois fais excepcion
Note that I don't include
Des patriarches et prophètes
The patriarchs and prophets
Car selon ma concepcion
According to my way of thinking
Onques n'eurent grant chault aux fesses.
These never got their asses burned[57]

Villon is here once again making reference to the ease with which the wealthy live their lives. However what interests us most here is his use of

---

[57] Kinnel, 76,77.

idiomatic language. The expression '*avoir chaud aux fesses*' from which this line '*n'eurent chault aux fesses*' derives is translated literally as to have a hot arse. In the *Littré*, one of Duchamp's preferred dictionaries, this expression is explained as '*avoir une chaude alarme*'. [58] This would generally be translated as to 'have a narrow escape', or more colloquially as translated by Galway Kinnel to get your arse burned.[59] The line and the expression '*avoir chaud aux fesses*' immediately brings to mind one of Duchamp's most famous 'works', his 1930 work *LHOOQ*, a pun using the pronunciation of letters to create a phrase. The letters when read out make the phrase *elle a chaud au cul*- literally 'she has a hot arse', meaning she is sexually aroused or

---

[58] *Littre*, (Paris : Librairie Hachette, et cie, 1883), 1651.
[59] Oxford Hachette for windows, entry for *fesse*, idioms.

arousing[60]. Here the use of almost the exact same expression as Villon's has a slightly different meaning, *avoir chaud aux fesses*, getting one's arse burned is slightly different from having a hot arse, as the word *cul* is more sexualised, than *fesses*. Porn and its industry is often referred to as *le cul.*[61] However the two expressions are closely related and share the same idiomatic and vulgar tone.

Villon continues in this tone in the closing stanzas of Testament:

---

[60] This expression is usually translated in studies of Duchamp literally as 'she has a hot arse', but as Elena Filipovic, *The Apparently Marginal Activities of Marcel Duchamp*, (Massachusetts: MIT Press, 2016) says it has not so much the idea of being sexually exciting but more the context of being sexually aroused i.e. 247 'her base corporeal desire'.

[61] François Caradec, *Dictionnaire du français argotique et populaire*, (Paris : Larousse, 2006), *68 le cul- 'aller au cul' aller faire l'amour, Le cul la pornographie et son industrie'.*

Icy clost le testament
Here ends and finishes
Et finist du pauvre Villon
the testament of poor Villon
Venez a son enterrement
Come to his burial
Quant vous orrez le carillon
When you hear the bell ringing
Vestus rouge com vermillon
Dressed in red vermillion
Car en amours mourant martir
For he died a martyr to love
Ce jura il sur son couillon
This he swore on his testicle
Quant de ce monde voulut partir
As he made his way out of this world[62]

The irreverence of swearing on one's testicle continues the erotic and vulgar tone of much of

---

[62] Kinnel, 152-153.

Villon's work, and in a fell swoop brings down to earth any lofty notions the idea of swearing an oath of truth may elicit. However, Villon's oath is honest. To Villon and many others their own testicles were probably more cherished than any text on which one might be asked to swear. Furthermore, rhyming *couillon,* testicle, with his own name, Villon, amplifies the humour, and, as noted by poet Louis Aragon, it leaves no doubt as to the pronunciation of his name, with a 'y' sound.

Villon uses a levelling of lofty ideals through language all through his oeuvre, which, even though in medieval French, is obvious to the modern reader.

To introduce the *Ballade aux pendus*, the poem which was so important for the Duchamp brothers, written when François Villon was condemned to death, he speaks in a very matter of fact manner of his condemnation and impending hanging

Je suis François, dont ce me poise,
I am François, which weighs on me
Né de Paris emprès Pontoise
Born in Paris near Pontoise.
Or d'une corde d'une toise
Now from a cord of six feet
Saura mon col que mon cul poise
My neck will know what my arse weighs.[63]

Despite the dire circumstances in which he finds himself Villon manages to make a joke about his origins: Paris is obviously nowhere near Pontoise, a much less significant town, and the matter of fact

---

[63] Gutenberg project, 101, 1881 Edition 101 also. My translation. A *toise* was a measure of around six feet. *Le nouveau Littré*, (Paris: Editions Garnier, 2005), 1736. The verb *toiser* means to measure up something or someone.

reference to the impending very physical weighing up of his metaphysical worth renders the verse comic in its reference to the weight of gravity.

Duchamp's attitude is similar, His acceptance with an ironic smile of the rejection of his work, Nude descending a Staircase #2, in 1912, shows his personal use of humour when faced with difficulty. Although he later said the Nu incident 'gave me a turn'[64] and that he would be completely independent from then on, his only direct response was an ironic smile.

Villon's use of assonance, in this particular instance, with the juxtaposition of *col* and *cul* adds to the comic tone of his verse. Assonance is a

---

[64] Pierre Cabanne, *Dialogues with Marcel Duchamp*, Da Capo Press, 1987, reprint of Thames and Hudson 1971 Edition, 17

device Duchamp often uses in his titles and in his puns and word games. In a discussion about what Duchamp believed, in *Interviews with Pierre Cabanne* Duchamp declares that he believes in 'nothing, of course', but that he likes 'word games. Assonances, Things like that... I like that very much'.[65] We have already mentioned Duchamp's love of word games and his 'work' *LHOOQ*, which spells out a vulgar phrase. It also exhorts one to LOOK, with a French accent. Of this work in particular Duchamp said 'I really like this kind of game, because I find that you can do a lot of them. But simply reading the letters in French, even in any language, some astonishing things happen. Reading the letters is very amusing'[66]

---

[65] Cabanne, 1987, 89-90

[66] Cabanne, 1987, 63

Villon is sensitive to the possibilities of rhyme with what could arguably be called Duchamp's favourite letter, R In the Ballade known as the *Ballade Pour Prier Notre Dame, Ballad to pray to Our Lady* Villon says, of love:

Ceste Ballade luy envoye,
This ballade I send to her
Qui se termine toute en R.[67]
Which ends all in R

He then uses the homophone of the letter R: the word *erre*- to wander, or to be mistaken, and uses the rhyme in the stanza, finishing the stanza by calling her 'Orde paillarde', a Dirty tramp[68]. The use of the R / erre homophone is common in

---

[67] *Œuvres completes*, 1881 Edition, 57. Grand Testament », huitaine LXXXIII,

[68] Champion, 146 *en errant c'est-à-dire en se trompant*. In erring, that is in being mistaken

French and, as evidenced by Villon's oeuvre, long standing. Duchamp plays with this letter in both French and English throughout his oeuvre. The French homophones of this letter is the word *aire*, air, erre/ wander or to err in judgement and its English homophone is the French word *art*, art.

This ballad is dedicated to Villon's former love Rose. Though it would be perhaps tenuous to suggest that Duchamp's choice of Rrose for the name of his alter ego, Rrose Selavy, invented in 1920, was inspired by these lines, the recollection of these lines may have brought an ironic smile to Duchamp's lips when he decided on Rrose's name. An oblique reference perhaps. Here Villon is bequeathing gifts:

LXXX.

Item, m'amour, ma chière Rose,
Item to my lover, my dear Rose
Ne luy laisse ne cuer ne foye:
I leave neither heart nor liver
Elle ameroit mieulx autre chose,
There's something she'd like even more
Combien qu'elle ait assez monnoye
And she isn't hard up for money
Quoy? une grant bource de soye,
What can it be ? A big silk purse,
Plaine d'escuz, parfonde et large:
Swollen with coins thick and long
Mais pendu soit il, que je soye
But may the man be hanged and me too
Qui luy laira escu ne targe
Who slips her his *écu* or his *targe*[69]

There is certainly an erotic overtone in both Villon's attitude to Rose and in Duchamp's Rrose. Villon speaks of Rose in clearly down to earth terms. The reference to the heart as much a flesh

[69]Kinnel, 82,85

and blood organ as a liver, and not a sentimental reference is clearly down to earth. The idea of slipping an *écu*, money of the time, or a *targe*, a shield, into her purse are clearly erotic[70]. This tone continues in the next stanza:

Car elle en a sans moy assez
For she gets it plenty without me
Mais de cela il ne m'en chault
But this doesn't rankle anymore
Mes plus grans dueilz en sont passez
My worst griefs have all gone by
Plus n'en ay le croppion chault
And I no longer get it up
SI m'en desmetz aux hoirs Michault
I stand aside for the heirs of Michault
Qui fut nommé le Bon Fouterre
Who was known as "The Great Fucker"
Priez pour lui, faites ung sault
Say a prayer for him, then go at it[71]

---

[70] *Le nouveau Littré*, *targe* p.1698
[71] Kinnell, 84,85

The unabashedly erotic tone of this stanza, and of much of Villon's work is also present in Duchamp's work. The addition of an R to the name of Duchamp's alter-ego *Rrose Selavy* is generally accepted as a reference to Eros, the god of sexual love. This gives, through a close homophone, *eros c'est la vie*, eros that's life. Any French person hearing Duchamp's alter ego's name Rrose Selavy would immediately think of the expression '*C'est la vie en rose'*, literally 'Its life in pink' which means to see things through rose coloured glasses. However, Duchamp, in adding the second R has turned this into seeing life through erotic glasses. He shares not only a significant phonic use of the letter R with Villon, but also a clearly down to earth erotic tone.

Another technique shared by both Villon and

Duchamp is the use of acrostics. In the same ballade cited above, Villon inserts his own first name.

Faulse beauté qui tant me couste chier
False beauty who makes me pay so dear
Rude en effect, ypicrite doulceur
Rude in fact pretending to be tender
Amour dure plus que fer a maschier
A love harder to chew than an iron bar
Nommer qui puis, de ma desfaçon seur
Now certain of my ruin I can name her
Cherme felon, la mort d'un povre cuer
Cozening thief, death of a heart so poor
Orgueil mussié qui gens met au mourir
Or secret pride, man's executioner
Yeulx sans pitié, ne veult Droit de Rigueur
Icy gaze, will not Justice with rigor
Sans empirer ung povre secourir ?
Save a poor man before he sinks under?[72]

In the next stanza Villon adds another acrostic, through it naming MARTHE. His own surname is contained in acrostic in the stanza preceding that

---

[72] Kinnell, 84-87

about his lover Rose. Hence Rose is, in this ballad, contained between Villon's names. Villon writes his name in acrostic several times in his oeuvre.

It is generally accepted that Duchamp used acrostics at least once in his oeuvre, in the title of his work, *Etant Donné, La mariée mise à nu par ses célibataires, même*. This translates as *Given, the wife stripped by her bachelors, even.* The elements of the **mar**iée and the **cél**ibataires are generally accepted as an acrostic of Duchamp's own name, Marcel.

A further acrostic exists in Duchamp's note to himself after the revelation of his last work *Etant Donné la chute d'eau, le gaz d'eclairage*. It betrays his anxiety about this final works' reception, despite his wish to always remain indifferent.

Dope- more ways than one

Ugly –

Contentious

Harlot, male

Arcane

Mentality of a deranged Teenager-

Pornographer[73]

[73] Thomas Zaunschirn, *Faux Vagin, Marcel Duchamp's Last Readymade*, Hatje Cantz, Ostfildern, 2014, 161, cited from Michael Taylor, *Exhibition Catalogue Etant Donnés*, Philadelphia Museum of Art new Haven and London, 2009, 174

5

Humour in the face of..

The use of humour continues all throughout Duchamp's oeuvre. Clearly, pretentiously calling a urinal "Fountain", as Duchamp famously did in 1917, and presenting it as a work of art was a provocative act intended to unmask the hypocrisy of the Society of Independent artists who had declared they would accept every entry submitted for their exhibition as art. His irreverence is palpable. Duchamp has no compunction about using scatological or vulgar humour in his art, nor did Villon. There are many examples of Villon using vulgar language in his work.

I include just a few as illustration. Towards the end of Villon's Grand Testament amongst those to whom he pleads for mercy are '*fillettes monstrans tetins*' 'young girls showing tits' and he frankly goes on to express his opinion of those who have made life difficult for him[74]:

Sinon aux trahistres chiens mastins,
Otherwise to treacherous guard dogs
Qui m'ont fait ronger dures crostes
Who made me eat hard crusts

---

[74] My translation of this line. Barbara Sargent Baur's translation in *Francois Villon Complete poems*, (Toronto: University of Toronto Press, 1994), of this line is 'of girls who wear their gowns cut low', 189, but in my opinion Villon's language is much more direct, and vulgar. I find most of her translations prudish and insensitive to Villon's use of different registers, most notably to his vulgar language. Galway Kinnel's translation *The poems of Francois Villon*, seems much more apt "Girls showing their breasts' 151. The *Dictionnaire hIstorique de la langue Française*, sous-direction d'Alain Rey, Le Robert, 2010, 2292, directs from the entry for *tetine* to the entry for *Tette* : '*probablement issue d'un germanique occidental titta, sein de femme, dont le radical tit a peut etre le sens de pointe*'. Probably from the western German *titta*, of which the radical *tit* perhaps has the meaning of point.

Et boire eau maintz soirs et matins,
And drink water many days and nights
Qu'ores je ne crains pas trois crottes.
Such that I don't fear three turds
Je feisse pour eulx petz et rottes;
I'd make for them farts and burps[75]

Duchamp's love of vulgar language and puns in his titles and works have been documented elsewhere: *Faucon/ faux con*: falcon /false cunt; and his

[75] Villon *Œuvres Completes*, 1881, 98. Grand testament, *Ballade par laquelle Villon crye mercy à chascun, Ballad for mercy*, Gutenberg, 98. Sargent Maur's translation of this is 'Except for those vile, treacherous dogs, / who caused me to gnaw on hard crusts/ And chew them many a night and day, / whom now I fear less than three turds/ I'd break wind for them and I'd belch. She uses a different text *Synon aux traitres chiens mastins/ qui m'ont fait ronger dures crostes,/ Macher mains soirs et mains matins,/ Je feisse pour eux pez et roctes.* Galway Kinnel uses yet another text based mostly on the Lognon-Foulet edition of 1932, *sinon aux traistres chiens matins' Qui m'ont fait chier dur et crostes/ Mascher mains soirs et mains crostes/Qu'ores je ne crains pas trois crotes/ je feisse pour eulx petz et rotes* translated as Except the sons of bitches / who made me shit small and gnaw/Crusts many a dusk and dawn/ who don't scare me now three turds/I'd raise for them farts and belches.

reference to Jarry's *merdre/merde*- shitte/shit to name a few. However, his use of puns and word games, which were considered a low form of humour, was considered gross by some. This even including such an unsophisticated young girl as his first wife Lydie Sarazin-Levassor, who, when still infatuated with him, detested his word games and puns and 'wondered how such a fine person could enjoy the heaviness of such gross jokes'[76] Duchamp himself admits that 'Puns are considered very low, low, low everywhere in English and in French.'[77]

---

[76] Lydie Fischer Sarazin Levassor, *Un Échec matrimonial, le cœur de la mariée mis à nu par son célibataire même*, (Dijon : Les presses du Réel, 2004), 47. Lydie is here lamenting Duchamps '*jeux de mots ou calembours que je détestais. Je me demandais toujours comment un être aussi fin pouvait se complaire dans la lourdeur de ces grossières plaisanteries.* ' 'word games or puns that I detested...'

[77] Duchamp, Tomkins, 2013, 90, here he is speaking about Roussel's punning 'not even a good pun'

If Duchamp was vilified by his peers, for the title of his works which was considered to be too literary and for making a nude descend a staircase instead of languishing seductively and passively before the viewer, as other nudes had done for centuries, Francois Villon chose to write of women who teased him and provoked him rather than to simply laud female virtues as had been the practice in poetry of the time with courtly verse, and as is the case with the poetry of his precursors including Charles d'Orléans. Indeed, Villon was convicted and whipped after insulting and probably writing unflattering verse about one of the women, Katherine de Vauselles, who had spurned him[78]. He recounts carrying out of this sentence in his *Double Ballade: J'en fus batu, comme à ru telles, / Tout*

[78] Jannet « Préface », *Les Oeuvres complètes de François Villon*, Ed. Marpon et Flammarion, Paris, 1881, ix.

nud jà ne le quiers celer. I was beaten, amply / Completely nude, that I don't wish to hide[79]

The *Double Ballade* is a complaint about the risks of love. One of the lines is: *"Folles amours font les gens bestes"* "Crazy loves make people stupid". It recounts the stories of historical or mythological male figures who have lost to love, and then speaks of Villon's own experience. Each verse ends with the refrain, *Bien Heureux est qui rien n'y a!* Happy is he who nothing of this has![80]

Duchamp's relationships with women were certainly cool and distant and his desire to remain unattached

[79] Villon *Oeuvres complètes, Grand testament, « Double ballade, sur le même propos »*, 1881 Ed, 46. Double ballade, on the same theme Barbara Sargent Baur's translation, 99: Beaten like laundry at a stream, / Nude I don't try to hide the fact. *Dictionnaire de L'ancien français, jusqu'au milieu du XIV siècle*, Larousse, par AJ Greimas, 1969, 574 a ru, à flots
[80] Villon, Les *Oeuvres Completes de FV*, 1881, 45.

is well documented. He seemed determined to keep a distance from women until late in life when he met and married his second wife, Teeny Matisse. His short-lived relationship with his first wife Lydie Sarazin Levassor, was seen as a marriage of convenience by her entourage who saw him as a *coureur de dot*, a dowry chaser. [81] The dowry turned out to be non-existant and the marriage was soon dissolved. He made sure his long-term relationship with the widow Mary Reynolds was kept secret and he refused to acknowledge her in public. Mary complained to Duchamp's friend Roche that he saw other women and was attracted to very vulgar women. [82] On Mary's death Duchamp received a pension from her family as they thought that's what

[81]Lydie Fischer Sarazin-Levassor, 35,51

[82] Susan S Glover « Cendres chaudes : vie et carrière de Mary Reynolds », *Etant Donné, no.8., Marcel Duchamp et Mary Reynolds*, 22

Mary would have wanted. He was still many years after their relationship had ended, exceedingly poor.

Duchamp, like Villon, experienced long-term poverty, though his response to it was vastly different from Villon's, and the reason for it was his fundamental opposition to the idea of working for a living, which he considered a "bêtise,' 'stupidity' 'Why do people have to work? Why do they think they have to work?"[83] 'Why should man work to live... the poor thing was put on earth without his permission to be here...on earth we have to work to breathe. I don't see why that's so admirable. I can conceive of a place where the lazies have a place in the sun.'... 'there was a book published in 1885 by one of the communist groups at that time. The name

[83] Duchamp in, Calvin Tomkins, 2013, 3.

of the book was "*The Right to Be Lazy*"'[84] . The fact that Duchamp remembered this book in 1964, is evidence of its impression on him during his youth. Duchamp also staunchly refused what he called the 'monetization of art', repetition of ideas and rapid production. Of his readymades he said 'There are only ten of them in my whole life. I could have been completely taken in by the idea.'[85] He then likens art to 'a habit forming drug'[86]. He insists on the value of slow production, rather than the rapid production that was taking place in the 1960s. "I really feel that things of great importance have to be slowly produced.'[87]

---

[84] Duchamp, Tomkins, 2013, 86, 87.
[85] Duchamp, Tomkins, 2013, 55
[86] Duchamp. Tomkins, 2013, 56.
[87] Duchamp, Tomkins, 2013, 26.

Of his readymades Duchamp said 'It was really to get out of the exchangeability, I mean the monetization...of the work of art. I never intended to sell my readymades... it was really a gesture to show that one could do something without having... the idea of making money through it.'[88] In his younger years Duchamp refused patronage. When offered a sizeable sum for his yearly output Duchamp refused, saying he immediately saw the danger. However, he did sell works by other artists to support himself. "my father died and I had some money...I bought a few Picabias, that I put into a sale... at the Hotel Drouot...I made a little money'[89] (Duchamp bought around 80 works from Picabia in 1925)[90] Though he calls dealers and collectors 'lice

[88] Duchamp, Calvin Tomkins, 2013, 26.
[89] Duchamp, Tomkins, 2013, 34
[90] Jennifer Gough Copper, Jacques Caumont, *Marcel Duchamp, Ephemerides*, MIT Press, Cambridge Massachusetts, 1993.

on the back of the artist' and 'parasites' he also made money from dealing in art.[91] Duchamp says there was very little money to make when he was selling art, but 'knowing all these people like Arp... I was tempted to buy things... for no other reason than that they needed some money, and then later on I would make a comparatively great profit on what I had bought.'[92] He did also sell editions of facsimiles of his readymades later in life through Galleria Schwarz[93], and he dealt in Brancusis.

If Duchamp's poverty was due to his status as an artist, who renounced art, Francois Villon's poverty was due to his poor background and his status as clerc which did not provide him with a regular

---

unpaginated, (ordered by dates), 1 Jan 1926, 28 Dec 1925.

[91] Duchamp., Tomkins, 2013, 33

[92] Duchamp in Calvin Tomkins, 2013, 34-35.

[93] This was probably in deference to Schwarz who idolized Duchamp, and spent many years producing his *Complete works of Marcel Duchamp*.

income. Villon came into contact with moneyed, influential people while at the *Université de Paris*, as there was a great inequality between the fortunes of the students.[94] But he also knew the language of tricksters, game fixers, lock pickers and thieves, and seems to have taken this path. *Je cognois quand pipeur jargonne.../Je cognois le vin à la tonne/ Je cognois tout*..I know when the game fixer speaks jargon/... I know wine by the tonne/ I know all[95] ...

However, in his Grand Testament, written in his older years, he admits having wasted his youth partying. *Je plaings le temps de ma jeunessse, / Ouquel j'ay plus qu'autre gallé. / Jusque à l'entrée de vieillesse.* I regret the time of my youth,/ When

[94] Champion, 35
[95] Poésies diverses, *Ballade de menus propos*, *Ballad of small comments*, line 13, Gutenberg, 118

I more than others partied./ Until the entry of old age.[96] Pierre Champion reads the continuation of this section of the Grand Testament as ironic: *Si ne crains avoir despendu / Par friander et par leschier; / par trop aimer n'ay riens vendu* If I don't fear having spent / with a taste for good things and debauchery[97] / by loving too much have nothing sold.[98] Champion states that Villon's friends should not have reproached his spending, as they enjoyed it as did Villon.[99]

Villon is aware that his own actions have led to the continuation of his poverty. He admits not studying

---

[96] *Œuvres de François Villon*, 1881, 27-28, huitaine XXII. My translation. Pierre Champion, 136, Champion translates *gallé* as *faire la noce*- to party.

[97] *Dictionnaire de l'Ancien Français Larousse*, 1969, 362 *leschier - être gourmand, débauché* Barbara Sargent Baur's translation *in Francois Villon Complete poems*, Univ Toronto Press, 1994, 65. Translates this as 'Yet I don't fear that I have spent much on feasting and on gluttony'

[98] "Grand Testament huitaine XXIV", Edition 1881, 28, my translation

[99] Pierre Champion, Vol II, 137.

Bien scay se j'eusse estudié
I well know that if I had studied
Ou temps de ma jeunesse folle
In the time of my mad youth
Et à bonne meurs dedié
And dedicated myself to good behaviour
J'eusse maison et couche molle!
I would have a house and soft bed!
Mais quoy? Je fuyoye l'escolle,
But what? I fled school
Comme faict le mauvays enfant...
As does the bad child
En escrivant ceste parole,
In writing these words
A peu que le coeur ne me fend
My heart nearly breaks[100]

As we can see, late in his life, Villon regrets his behaviour and advises against following the kind of life he has had. One section of his Grand Testament

[100] "Grand Testament huitaine XXVI", Edition 1881, 29, my translation

is known as the *Ballade de Bonne Doctrine, The Ballad of Good Doctrine*. In this Villon advises that if one leads a *mauvaise vie*, a bad life, then all that one gains, whether from gambling, theatre or from labouring the fields, will go *Tout aux Tavernes et aux Filles, All to the Taverns and Girls*. This line ends several stanzas of this ballad.

6

Thirst and the Fountain[101]

One of François Villon's *Ballades*, known as The *Ballade du concours de Blois* begins with a line from Charles D'Orleans: *Je meurs de soif aupres de la Fontaine*, I die of thirst beside the Fountain. The *Concours de Blois* was a competition in which poets had to use this line as the first line of their poem. [102] Hence a

[101] This chapter is also produced in my *Marcel Duchamp's Fountain in Context: Readymades Read and Made, Part 2.*
[102] For Charles D'Orléans see Poesie.webnet.fr/lesgrandesclassiqeus/Poemes/Charlesd-orleans/je_meurs_de_soif_en_couste_la_fontaine

tradition of paradox and contradiction was already well established, even institutionalized from the 15th century. Duchamp is firmly placed in this tradition, the lineage, tracing through his brothers who chose to name themselves after Francois Villon, to Marcel.

Villon's poem is in 3 equal verses with a refrain in the last line, following the form of Charles d'Orlean's poem. Villon's ballade, like that of D'Orléans contains a series of contradictions:

Je meurs de soif aupres de la fontaine,
I die of thirst beside the fountian
Chault comme feu et tremble dent a dent
I'm hot as fire, I'm shaking tooth on tooth
En mon Païs suis en terre loingtaine
In my own country I'm in a distant land

Lez ung brasier frissonne tout ardent
Beside the blaze I'm shivering in flames
Nu comme ung ver, vestu en president

Naked as a worm dressed like a president
Je ris en pleurs et attens sans Espoir
I laugh in tears and hope in despair
Confort reprens en triste desespoir
I cheer up in sad hopelessness
Je m'esjouis et n'ay plaisir aucun
I'm joyful and no pleasure's anywhere
Puissant je suis sans force et sans povoir
I'm powerful and lack all force and strength
Bien recueully, debouté de chascun
Warmly welcomed always turned away

Rien ne m'est seur que la chose uncertain
I'm sure of nothing but what is uncertain
Obscur, fors ce qui est tout evident
Find nothing obscure but the obvious
Doubte ne fais fors en chose certain
Doubt nothing but the certainties

Science tiens a soudain accident
Knowledge to me is a mere accident
Je gaigne tout et demeure perdent
I keep winning but remain the loser

Au point du jour dis "Dieu vous doint bon soir"
At dawn I say "I bid you good night"
Gisant envers j'ay grant paour du cheoir
Lying down I'm afraid of falling
J'ay bien de quoy et si n'en ay as ung
I'm so rich but haven't a penny
Eschoitte attens et d'omme ne suis hoir
I await an inheritance and am no-one's heir
Bien recueully, debouté de chascun
Warmly welcomed, always turned away.

De Riens n'ay soing si mectz toute ma paine
I never work and yet I labour
D'acquerir biens et n'y suis pretendent
To acquire goods I don't even want
Qui mieulx me dit c'est cil qui plus m'attaine
Kind words irritate me the most

Et qui plus vray lors plus me va bourdent
He who speaks true deceives me the most
Mon amy est qui me fait entendent
A friend is someone who makes me think
D'un cigne blanc que c'est ung corbeau noir

A white swan is a black crow
Et qui me nuyst croy qu'il m'ayde a povoir
The people who harm me think they help
Bourde, verté, au jour d'uy m'est tout un
Lies and truth today I see they're one
Je retiens tout , rien ne scay concepvoir I
remember everything my mind's a blank
Bien recueully, debouté de chascun
Warmly welcomed, always turned away

Prince clement, or vous plaise sçavoir
Merciful Prince may it please you to know
Que j'entens moult et n'ay sens ne sçavoir
I understand much and have no wit or learning
Parcial suis a toutes loys commun
I am biased against all laws impartially

Que fais je plus?Quoy? Les gaiges ravoir
What's next to do? Redeem my pawned goods
again
Bien recueully, debouté de chascun
Warmly welcomed, always turned away[103]

Villon's contradictions and paradox is essential to any understanding of Duchamp's French heritage. Many of these particular lines from François Villon could have been written in reference to Marcel in his new life in the United States. Marcel was certainly aware of Francois Villon's work, and had internalised his spirit of contradiction and provocation.

'I die of thirst beside the Fountain'

Certainly one would die of thirst bedside

[103] Kinnell, 176-179

Marcel's Fountain. His reorienting of the urinal by laying it on its back and renaming it ensured this.

'In my own country I'm in a distant land.'

He had adopted the United States as his own home

'I laugh in tears and hope in despair'.

Marcel's ironic laughter was a reaction to his brothers Villon and his peers rejection of his artwork in 1912 and the committee of the independents in 1917, and his hope may have been in despair.

'I cheer up in sad hopelessness'.

Gabrielle Buffet Picabia's description of him reflects such an attitude 'despite the pitiless pessimism of his mind, he was personally delightful with his gay ironies'[104]

'I'm sure of nothing but what is uncertain

Find nothing obscure but the obvious

Doubt nothing but the certainties'

Much of Duchamp's oeuvre is based on doubt, and doubt of what others considered to be certainties, such as definitions.

He said: 'Anything is dubious. It's pushing the idea of doubt of Descartes, you see, to a much further point than they ever did in the School of Cartesianism: Doubt in myself, doubt in everything. In the first place never believing in truth. In the end, you come to doubt "being".[105]

---

[104] Gabrielle Buffet-Picabia, cited from Robert Motherwell, *The Dada Poets and Painters*, (New York , George Wittenborn Inc, 1951), 259,260.

[105] *Marcel Duchamp, Paroles D'artistes*, (Paris, Fage Editions,

I am biased against all laws impartially.

Gabrielle Buffet Picabia's description speaks of 'his contempt for all values, even the sentimental'[106]

The late night chess games and partying at Arensberg's home may have led to a similar sentiment to that of Francois Villon's:

At dawn I say "I bid you good night"

'Lying down I'm afraid of falling',

as one would be if drunk,

And Marcel's good fortune in finding the Arensbergs as patrons is reflected in the following line:

'I'm so rich but haven't a penny'

2018), 24. from Interview with William Seitz, 'What's happened to Art' originally published in *Vogue*, New York, 15 February, 1963

[106] Gabrielle Buffet Picabia in Motherwell, 259.

‘I never work and yet I labour’
Duchamp didn’t ‘work’ a regular job but laboured on his art, though not to acquire goods, as Villon had.

Certainly Duchamp would have concurred with Villon in saying
‘A friend is someone who makes me think’
The relevance of these lines of Francois Villon’s to Duchamp’s life demonstrates the importance of his particular French heritage, which celebrated the vulgar, the commonplace and the larrikin, throwing doubt on institutions and parodying their forms and their thinking.

7

Testament and signs

Villon's humour is present in both his Testaments. The testament was a common form of poetry at the time and was written when a long voyage was about to be undertaken or in times of uncertainty. He wrote two testaments which are known as the *Petit Testament* or the *Lais*, and the *Grand Testament*. Villon follows the general form of this poetry, praying to the virgin, making arrangements for payment of debts, instructions for the inhumation of the body, appointment of executors, and bequests of all his worldly goods, but his bequests are mostly jokes, and his use of the form has been called a parody. It would have been quite evident at the time that he wrote them that his bequests were jokes to a public who knew the people to whom he was bequeathing his worldly goods[107]. For example in his *Petit Testament (Le Lais)* he left to Robert Vallée, a rich lawyer, some *brayes*[108], - his underpants, which were to be found at the t*rummelières, high boots*-the name of a tavern which was near Les Halles at the time.[109] One often left one's clothes as security for a debt, but one should never leave ones underpants.[110]

---

[107] Champion, Vol. II, 181

[108] *Dictionnaire de l'ancien Français*, (Paris : Larousse, 1969) 81 *Braie n. f. XII lat . pop d'orig gaul) Ample culotte serrée aux jambes par des lanières, XII ceinture des braies, ceinture , taille. 647 trumeliere n.f. (XIIIe s.,) Jambiere*

[109] *Oeuvres De FV*, 1881, Petit Testament, huitaine XIV, 11.

[110] Pierre Champion, Vol. II, 22

Villon left them '*Pour coeffer plus honestement / S'amye Jehanneton de Millières.* To cover more suitably the head of / His friend Jehanetton De Millieres. The insinuation is that he thought Vallee's wife wore the britches in the family. Clearly thinking him stupid he also left him a ridiculous work the *L'Art de mémoire* which was to be found at *Malpensé,* (Badly Theorised's house), another pun[111].

Villon continues his comments on the character of many of his legatees in his *Grand Testament.* He calls Jehan de la Garde Jehan Thibaud because Thibaud was the patron saint of betrayed husbands.[112] He continues this verse, thinking of Genvoys, who describes ironically as having a

---

[111] Champion, Vol. II, 22

[112] Champion, 160.

beautiful nose from drinking from the barrel.[113]

Many other bequests can still be seen to be evidently jokes, many of which are based on the sculpted signs that hung outside rich bourgeois' houses and other businesses in Paris at the time. His testaments show a topography of Paris through the signs which he jokingly bequests to particular people in his Testaments[114]. For example, in his *Petit Testament* he leaves to the butcher Jehan Trouvé, the signs from *le Mouton, le Boeuf Couronné et La Vache,* the Sheep, the Crowned Beef, and the Cow, These were the names of Taverns at the time. To a rich draper, Jacques Cardon, evidently a glutton, he leaves a legacy

---

[113] *Oeuvres de Francois Villon*, 1881, Grand Testament, huitaine CXXVII, 73. both Jehan de la Garde, and Genevoys Et plus beau nez a pour y boyre.
[114] Gaston Paris, topography, 30.

that is worth nothing, and also orders him to eat every day a fat goose, a fat chicken, and to drink '*10 muids de vin diuretique, blanc comme la craie*', (10 x 268 litres) of diuretic wine, white as chalk; to the good drinker Jacques Raguier- he left the *Abreuvoir Popin*, Popin's Watering place, on the Seine where horses were taken to drink, and he leaves him peaches and pears at the *Gros figuier*, Fat Figtree, *'une tavern sans doute'*; To his barber, his shoemaker, and his tailor, he leaves the cutting from his hair, his old shoes and his old clothes, "*Pour moins qu'ilz me cousteraient neufz /Charitablement je leur laisse*' " for less than they would cost me new ; / Charitably I leave them to them'[115]

[115] Champion, Tome II, 23-29. *Œuvres de FV*, 1881, Petit Testament Jacques Cardon huitaine XVII, 12 ; Jacques Raguyer, huitaine XX,13 ; barber, shoemaker, tailor, huitaine,

In his Grand Testament Villon continues along these lines leaving bequest that are either ironic, as the people to whom they were destined very evidently already had such things, and much more, or made to highlight the particular person's weaknesses. One of first legacies in this testament is to his *'plus que père'* 'more than father' Guillaume de Villon, whose name he took and who "*Dejetté m'a de maint bouillon*' 'Steered me away from many troubles'[116]. To him he leaves his library, mentioning specifically *le Rommant du Pet au Deable, The Tale of the Devil's Fart.*[117] This is evidently not the type of book an upstanding

XXXI, 16

[116] *FV œuvres complètes*, Grand Testament, v LXXVII, LXXVIII, 1881 ed.53-54

[117] A *rommant* was a form of poem in ancient style not necessarily a *roman*, a novel, as we understand it today. Kinnell, 81.

of the title of this book.

person such as Guillaume de Villon would have liked to receive. Gaston Paris claims it was Villon's own work, now lost.

The *Pet au Deable* was the name given to an unusual, vessel shaped large stone which was suspended in front of Mme de Bruyères' private hotel in Paris at the time, which probably took its name from *'un vieux et sale fabliaux bien connu a Paris'* 'an old and dirty fable well known in Paris', told by Rutebeuf.[118] The book the *Pet au Deable* recounted the events of 1451 when the *écoliers de Paris*, the students of the *Université de Paris* stole the stone from in front of the hotel, moved it to Montagne st Genevieve, in the street Mont Saint Hilaire, near the colleges, decorated it, danced

[118] Champion, Vol.II, 54.

around it and 'worshipped it'[119]. They required passersby to pledge allegiance to it in a farcical ceremony.[120] The word *Hilaire* is a near homophone of the French word '*hilare*', 'hilarious, laughing'. The students created a series of farces with the signs that were placed outside rich bourgeois hotels, taverns and other businesses at the time. These farcical actions were based on *jeux de mots*, word games, made with the signs.

The text of the Roman du *Pet au Deable* is lost, however another medieval text gives us an idea of what it may have been like. It recounts how students stole the signs from the *Cardinal de la Pierre au Lait, The Cardinal of the milk stone, and*

---

[119] Champion, Vol II, 61-64.

[120] Gaston Paris, 26. Paris does not mention specifically Mont Sainte Hilaire. But does have an account of the theft of the stone and the students' actions.

the Prescheur du cheuet Saint Jacques, Preacher of St Jacques' bedside for a mock ceremony to marry the signs from la *Truie* et *l'Ours*, the Sow and the Bear.

To make their bread, tartes, flans and pastes '*nous prendrons le Four Gauquelon en la rue l'arbre sec, en prendrons nostre Queux [chef] en Galendre... pour cuire nostre viande nous prendrons le chaudron en la Viez Monnoie... les Paelles au bout de la rue aux Parcheminiers, Le Pot de cuivre..., le Gril en la Mortelerie* etc etc « We will take the *Gauquelin Oven* in the street of the dry tree, and will take our *Chef* from Galendre... to cook our meat we'll take the *Cauldron* from Old Money, the *Paellas*, from the end of Parchment street, the

Copper Pot... the *Grill* from la mortelerie' etc.[121]

Although it is uncertain whether Duchamp knew the details of the story, he would certainly have grasped the comic nature of the name of the *Rommant le Pet au Deable*, the *Poem the Devils Fart*, and its unsuitability as a bequest for someone such as Guillaume de Villon. He probably appreciated the irony of the upstanding Guillaume de Villon being remembered as the patron of François Villon, larrikin, criminal, and poet. It is possible Duchamp may have known some of the details of Villon's comic use of signs, as Gaston Paris 1910 study does recount the story of the *Pet au Deable* and notes Villon's penchant for jokes

---

121 *François Villon sa vie et son temps, Tome I*, 62. Bibl nat., ms. Lat 4641 B fol 148 (*stylus curiae Parlament*); au fol.150 le dit rimé contre Hugues Aubriot. - cette pièce publie par A Jubinal , *Mystères XVe siecle*, 369-376.

with signs in his *Testaments*, considering the story of the *Pet au Deable* to be important to Villon's development. In any case Marcel Duchamp's work can be seen as belonging to a very long tradition of word games and jokes, of which Villon was a primary vulgar exponent.

Duchamp's uses signs several times in his oeuvre. The first instance is in 1918, when he uses a signwriter for part of the creation of his work *Tu m'*. This was a commission for Catherine Dreier, which he reluctantly undertook. The title is generally understood to be an underhand insult, meaning 'You ...me', one being able to insert a word beginning with a vowel, and the word which most comes to mind, and the one suggested by several Duchamp commentators being *emmerdes*. This literally means 'You give me the shits' or translated in a more polite manner 'You annoy me.' An unstated declaration of annoyance. The title of this work may also be read as a reference to Catherine Drier's feeling for Duchamp. The question one asks about this title is "What comes after you / *tu*? The response being simply 'm'. As the letter 'm' is a homophone of the word *'aimes'* to love, the title of this work can be read as an unstated declaration by Duchamp of his awareness of Dreir's love for him.

"Tu m" is a kind of summary of all Duchamp's works prior to the date of its creation, however what interests us here is Duchamp's use of signage. He has a sign writer paint a hand pointing to the right. Significantly this part of the work is signed, by the sign writer A Klang[122]. Here it is almost

---

[122] Karl Gerstner, *Marcel Duchamp: Tu m' Puzzle upon puzzle*,

impossible not to think of the idiomatic expression in English 'And the penny drops with a clang'[123]. The significance of this expression is that it emphasises the importance of sound in conveying and echoing meaning and emphasises the idea that something that is patently obvious is finally understood. The *Macmillan Dictionary of Unconventional English* 'Penny's dropped ...or the penny'll drop in a minute. A catch phrase to mark the belated appreciation of humour.'[124] The choice of this name and hence this expression by Duchamp surely highlights the humorous nature of this work

---

(Ostfildern Ruit, Ed. Hatje Cantz Verlag, 2003), 25. Gerstner makes no reference to the expression 'the penny drops with a clang', nor does any other commentator to my knowledge. Several other commentators have however identified Klang as the author of the painted hand.

[123] *Dictionnaire Francais anglais, Senior,* (Paris, Glasgow: Robert Collins) 2002, 1847, entry for penny, *ça a fait tilt,*

[124] Eric Partridge, *A Dictionary of Slang and Unconventional English, 8th edition, Colloquialisms and Catchphrases, Solecisms, Catachreses, Nicknames and Vulgarisms,* (New York: Macmillan, 1984), 868.

and shows *Tu m'* to be truly of its time. The A. Klang / a clang, surely highlights the resounding echo of delayed comprehension. The importance of this name can be supported by the fact that other elements in this work were painted by third parties for Duchamp but were not signed by them.[125] The evocation of this expression also carries on from the toilet humour of the *Fountain*, as the expression 'the penny drops (with a clang)' is also linked with the introduction of slot payment or the expression to 'spend a penny' in public toilets. The first paid public toilets were introduced by the magician John Maskelyne in London in the late nineteenth century and in the United States the first paid toilets were introduced

[125] Gertstner, 25. The row of rhombuses were painted by Yvonne Chastel.

in 1910[126]. It is quite probable that there was some press about the introduction of this newfangled idea from England, and the expressions it engendered. Duchamp's sensitivity to expressions and vernacular language makes it extremely likely that he would have picked up on this and been amused by it.

Duchamp's use of word games in this work is typical of his technique.

The second instance of Duchamp's use of signs is in 1923 with his poster *Wanted.* This work is in the form of a wanted poster complete with mug shots

---

126 https://wikipedia.org/wiki/John_Nevil_Maskelyne 21/04/2018, cited from Peter Lamont, *The Rise of the Indian Rope trick, The biography of a Legend*, 1 ed, 2004 Time Warner Books, ISBN 0-316-72430-0. For first public toilet https://en.wikepedia.org/wiki/Public_toilet#cite_note-first-58 21/04/2018 cited from Gruenstein, Peter, (4 Sept 1975) "Pay toilet movement attacks capitalism" *The Beaver County Times* retrieved Oct 19 2010.

of Marcel and text as follows: 'For information leading to the arrest of George C Welch, alias Bull, Alias Pickens etcetry. Etcetry. Operated Bucket Shop in New York under name Hook Lyon and Cinquer. Height about 5 feet nine inches. Weight about 190 pounds, complexion medium, eyes same. Known also under the name Rrose Selavy'.

The puns in this abound, 'welch' meaning 'to swindle'; 'bull' meaning to have intercourse with a woman', 'to mock' and 'to cheat'; and pickens being a near homophone of 'pickings', meaning 'pilferings'.[127] Duchamp is evidently doing all the above, and showing why he was 'wanted' in several senses of the word. A bucket shop was an American

---

[127] Eric Partridge, *The Routledge Dictionary of Historical Slang*, (London: Routledge & Kegan Paul, 1973), 'welch' 1034, 'bull 126; *Oxford English reference Dictionary*, (Oxford: Oxford University Press, 1995), pickings 1096

name for 'an unauthorised office for the sale of stocks', and Hook Lyon and Cinquer are obvious near homophones to 'hook, line and sinker' meaning 'completely, utterly' often used in the idiomatic expression 'to fall for something hook line and sinker'.[128] For the expression 'fall for something hook line and sinker' the French would say '*avaler... [quelquechose] sans questions*', without questions.[129] Evidently Duchamp is here poking fun at those who do just this and fall for his jokes in this way.

The third instance of Duchamp's use of signs is on the deluxe Editions of the cover of Robert Lebel's

---

[128] *Routledge Dictionary of Historical slang*, 'bucket shop' 122, 'hook line and sinker' 454.; *Hachette-Oxford Dictionary for Windows*, 'fall for something hook, line and sinker', entry for 'sinker'.

[129] François Denoeu, David Sices, Jacqueline Sices, *2001 French and English Idioms 2nd Edition 2001 Idiotismes français et Anglais,* (Hauppage, New York: Barrons Educational Series, 1996, 559.

1959 monograph about him *Sur Marcel Duchamp*. The publication of this book was fraught with problems and took much longer than anticipated. Lebel decided to write the book in 1949 and began work on it in the mid-50s before he had a publisher. Originally with Trianon Fawcus Publications, it was envisaged to take around a year to complete. However, there were problems with the Editor, the finance, the photographs, the text and the translation, which considerably delayed publication. The book was originally intended to be financed by Editor Arnold Fawcus through interested parties and his own contribution, however costs ballooned, the project stalled, and it was finally published by Trianon Press. Amongst other problems Fawcus misplaced Lebel's text for some time and Lebel, ever the perfectionist, often added details or even chapters to be inserted after it was supposed to be completed. Acquiring quality reproductions of some of the works became difficult and time consuming. Given the mercurial nature of the text, finding a translator became difficult. The first translation by Wernick was abandoned for a second one by Richard Hamilton, despite Fawcus' unhappiness with Hamilton's style and, significantly, his limited knowledge of French idioms. Hamilton was 'sure to be on time', and this took precedence. The process of the publication of Lebel's work has been amply detailed by Paul B Franklin in the journal *Etant Donné*[130].

Lebel's book on Duchamp was produced in a trade edition and a deluxe Edition. The deluxe Edition

[130]Paul B Franklin, "1959 Headline, Duchamp", *Etant Donné Marcel Duchamp*, (Paris : Association pour l'etude de Marcel Duchamp, 2006), no.7, 140-175.

had a sign on the cover. The inscription was '*EAU ET GAZ A TOUS LES ETAGES*', which translates literally as WATER AND GAS AT ALL LEVELS' [or STAGES]. This type of sign was common on buildings which were fully serviced with these amenities in the early twentieth century. The use of this sign is, to my mind, Duchamp's ironic tongue in cheek comment on the problems that occurred with the publication of this book. No-one to my knowledge has made note of this sign and its relation to the expression '*Il y a de l'eau dans le gaz*', literally 'there is some water in the gas', meaning the presence of water in the gas inhibits the smooth running of a machine or a car, or, more generally, 'there is a problem' something's afoot, or people aren't getting on well together[131]. So

---

[131] I owe my discovery of this expression to Jean-Pierre Descamps who used it in everyday speech.

'EAU ET GAZ A TOUS LES ETAGES' can be translated as "PROBLEMS AT ALL STAGES". We can imagine Duchamp liking this expression as it brings up an image of a machine spluttering along inefficiently. This was no doubt a popular expression in his youth when machines, particularly cars, were beginning to be part of everyday life.

The fourth instance of the use of a sign in Duchamp's 'oeuvre' is with his *Signed Sign*, a 'readymade' which Duchamp signed when it was presented to him whilst he was staying at the Hotel Green in October 1963 for his first major retrospective exhibition, which was held at the Pasadena Art Gallery. This exhibition was entitled *Of or By Marcel Duchamp or Rrose Selavy.* The title literally indicated Duchamp's love of wordplay and his sensitivity to the vagaries of translation, '*de*' in

French being translated either as 'of', 'from', or 'by' in English. Furthermore, his choice to stay at the Hotel Green tickled Duchamp's fancy, the Green recalling his love of *langue verte*, slang or literally green language, and highlighting the green thread that traces through Duchamp oeuvre.

When asked about the significance of the colour Green, Duchamp said "I have nothing much to say about it... it comes back to interior decoration and probably some taste there.' [132] Once again Duchamp leaves much unstated. The many instances of the use of green in Duchamp's oeuvre, from his early landscapes to the coloring of his *Boite Verte*, the *Green Box* of 1934, have been noted by many, including Paul Franklin. He also

[132] Walter Hopps and Dennis Hopper "A readymade in the making" *Etant Donné, Marcel Duchamp, Marcel Duchamp and John Cage*, no.6, 184.

mentions the homonym of the French *vert / verre*, green / glass, with reference to the Large Glass. I would also note the homonym *vers,* verse or lines of poetry which traverses his oeuvre. Hopper and Hopps, also in *Etant Donné* note the importance of the color Green in Duchamp's oeuvre[133].

This readymade *Signed Sign* coincidentally contained a hand indicating the direction towards the Hotel Green which recalled the pointing hand painted by A Klang in Duchamp's earlier work *Tu m'*. The sign was stolen by Dennis Hopper and Duchamp signed it 'Marcel Duchamp/Pasadena 1963', along the extended index finger and thumb of the hand on the sign. Hopper says, 'I had long quoted Duchamp's idea that the artist of the future would not paint but merely point his finger and say

[133] Hopps and Hopper, 186.

"that object is art" and it would be art."[134]

Once again Duchamp merely indicates the way, and leaves enunciation up to others, giving them a role to play in the completion and interpretation of his art.

[134] Hopps and Hopper, 186.

Conclusion

There are certainly many commonalities between the work of Francois Villon and Marcel Duchamp. Their love of the vernacular or of *langue verte,* green language, and their use of humour in the face of adversity set them apart from many other artists. It seems Duchamp's exposure to Francois Villon at the turning point in his life was certainly not insignificant for his future direction. Certainly, Marcel shares more the larrikin and punning *esprit*, wit or spirit of Francois Villon than do his namesake brothers. Francois Villon is a very important figure in Duchamp's life who has certainly not been taken into account in the Anglophone literature on Duchamp and has perhaps been taken for granted in Francophone circles, his influence on Marcel not having been explored.

Selected Bibliography

Cabanne, *Pierre, Dialogues with Marcel Duchamp*, (New York: Da Capo Press, 1987), reprint of Thames and Hudson 1971 Edition

Cabanne, *Pierre, The Brothers Duchamp*, (Boston, New York Graphic society, 1976)

Champion, Pierre, *François Villon sa vie et son temps,* (Paris: Honore Chapion, 1913)

Duchamp, Marcel *Marcel Duchamp: Paroles D'artistes*, (Paris: Fage Editions, 2018)

Filipovic, Elena, *The Apparently Marginal Activites of Marcel Duchamp*, (Massachusetts: MIT Press, 2016)

Gerstner, Karl, *Marcel Duchamp: Tu m' Puzzle upon puzzle*, (Ostfildern Ruit: Ed. Hatje Cantz Verlag, 2003)

Gough Cooper, Jennifer, Caumont, Jacques, *Marcel Duchamp Work and Life*, (Cambridge,

Massachusetts: MIT Press, 1993) (*Ephemerides*)

Jannet, Pierre, *Oeuvres Complètes de François Villon*, (Paris: Marpon et Flammarion, 1881)

Kinnel, Galway, *The Poems of Francois Villon*, (Hanover, London: University of New England Press, 1977)

Merrington, Lyn, *Marcel Duchamp's Fountain in Context: Readymades Read and Made Part 2*, (Perth: Are Press, 2020)

Motherwell, Robert, *The Dada Poets and Painters*, (New York: George Wittenborn Inc, 1951)

Paris, Gaston, *Les Grands Ecrivains Français, François Villon*, (Paris : Librairie Hachette, 1910)

Sarazin Levassor, Lydie Fischer, *Un Échec matrimonial, le cœur de la mariée mis à nu par son célibataire même*, (Dijon: Les presses du Réel, 2004)

Sargent Baur, Barbara, *Francois Villon Complete poems*, (Toronto: University of Toronto Press,

1994)

Tomkins,Calvin, *Duchamp, a Biography*, (New York: Henry Holt and Company, 1996)

Tomkins, Calvin, *Marcel Duchamp, The Afternoon Interviews*, (New York: Badlands Unlimited, 2013)

Zaunschirn, Thomas, *Faux Vagin, Marcel Duchamp's Last Readymade*, (Ostfildern: Hatje Cantz, 2014)

Dictionaries:

Caradec, François, *Dictionnaire du français argotique et populaire*, (Paris: Larousse, 2006)

Denoeu, François, Sices, David, Sices, Jacqueline, *2001 French and English Idioms 2nd Edition 2001 Idiotismes français et Anglais*, (Hauppage, New York: Barrons Educational Series, 1996)

Dictionnaire de l'ancien français, jusqu'au milieu du XLVe siecle, (Paris: Larousse, 1969)

Dictionnaire Francais anglais, Senior, (Paris,

Glasgow: Robert Collins 2002)

Le Nouveau Littré, (Paris: Editions Garnier, 2005)

Littre, (Paris : Librairie Hachette, et cie, 1883)

Partridge, Eric, *The Routledge Dictionary of Historical Slang*, (London: Routledge & Kegan Paul, 1973),

Oxford English reference Dictionary, (Oxford: Oxford University Press, 1995),

Partridge, Eric, *A Dictionary of Slang and Unconventional English, 8th edition, Colloquialisms and Catchphrases, Solecisms, Catachreses, Nicknames and Vulgarisms*, (New York: Macmillan, 1984)

Articles

Franklin, Paul B, “1959 Headline, Duchamp”, *Etant Donné Marcel Duchamp*, (Paris: Association pour l’Étude de Marcel Duchamp, 2006), no.7, 140-175

Glover Susan S, « Cendres chaudes : vie et carrière

de Mary Reynolds », *Etant Donné, Marcel Duchamp et Mary Reynolds* (Paris: Association pour l'Étude de Marcel Duchamp, 2007) *no.8,* 22

Hopps, Walter, Denis Hopper, Dennis, 'A readymade in the making', *Etant Donné, Marcel, Duchamp and John Cage*, (Paris: Association pour l'Étude de Marcel Duchamp, 2005) no.6, 184

Lancien, Catherine, Loisel, Carole, Musées de la vile de Rouen, Photograph from *Etant Donné,* (Paris : Association pour l'etude de Marcel Duchamp, 2006) *no. 6 Marcel Duchamp et John Cage*, Paris, 2005, 5

Merrington, Lyn, 'Marcel's Blagues', *Australian and New Zealand Journal of Art*, Vol20 Issue 2, 2020 upcoming https://doi.org/10.1080/14434318.2020.1837372

Perlman, B. Bennard "Font of inspiration" *Art and Antiques*, Sept 2005, vol. 28 Issue 9, 70-73.

Web references

https://wikipedia.org/wiki/John_Nevil_Maskelyne 21/04/2018, cited from Peter Lamont, *The Rise of the Indian Rope trick, The biography of a Legend*, 1 ed, 2004 Time Warner Books, ISBN 0-316-72430-0. For first public toilet https://en.wikepedia.org/wiki/Public-_toilet#cite_note-first-58 21/04/2018 cited from Gruenstein, Peter, (4 Sept 1975) "Pay toilet movement attacks capitalism" *The Beaver County Times* retrieved Oct 19 2010.

For Charles D'Orléans see Poesie.webnet.fr/lesgrandesclassiqeus/Poemes/Charlesdorleans/je_meurs_de_soif_en_couste_la_-fontaine

ABOUT THE AUTHOR

Lyn Merrington is an Australian artist and art historian with a profound interest in French culture, language and art history. She has visited major Duchamp sites in the United States, France and Spain, and has made in depth studies of the major literary figures which Duchamp considered important. She believes in the importance of historical and cultural contextualization, and above all linguistic proficiency in any cultural study, especially in regard to Duchamp who repeatedly cited the importance of language in relation to his oeuvre. And then there is humour...

www.ingramcontent.com/pod-product-compliance
Lightning Source LLC
LaVergne TN
LVHW010624100826
845148LV00014B/3103

9780648727644